Best Friends
Adult Coloring
Book

Animals, Nature Patterns and Mandalas to Color with
Touching and Humorous Quotes about Best Friends

To

Love,

I hope we grow old together, but I hope your boobs sag first.

I love you more than wine, and that's a lot.

Best friends are like the perfect bra - hard to find but always there to support you!

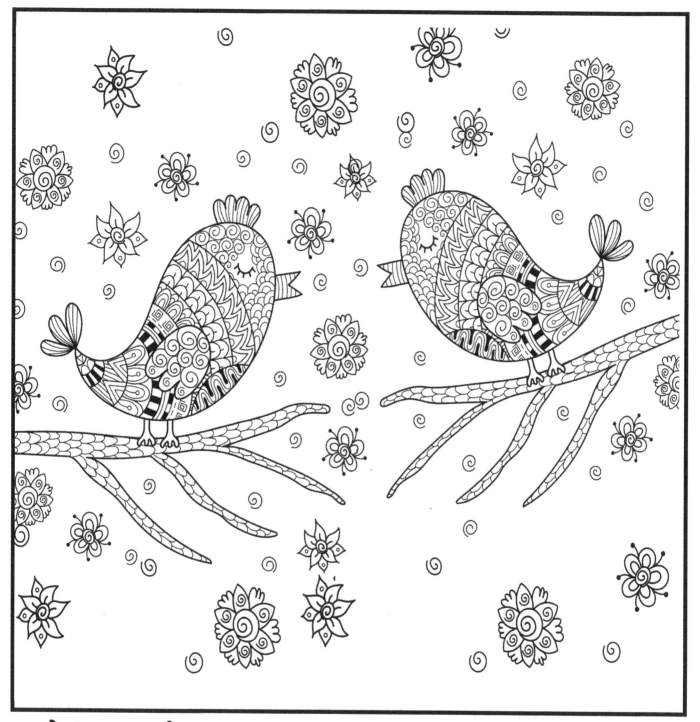

When I swear not to tell anyone, ever...of course it doesn't include my best friend!

I will always be there to pick you up if you fall...right after I stop laughing.

Your best friend helps you forget the past, enjoy the present and look forward to the future.

Your best friend is better than a therapist. She'll listen to your problems and then make you laugh about them!

A friend is one that knows you as you are, understands where you have been, accepts what you have become, and still, gently allows you to grow.

- William Shakespeare

Your best friend will tell you "don't worry, no one will notice", even when you both know it's not true.

When I count my blessings,
I count you twice!

Your best friend hears you even when you are silent.

A Best Friend will let you borrow their phone, even if there is only 2% battery life left.

Best Friends don't let you do stupid things...by yourself.

Best Friends are never apart, Sometimes in distance, but never at heart.

Made in the USA
Columbia, SC
13 December 2019